How to play hymns and gospel songs in evangelistic style.

by David Carr Glover · Phyllis Gunther

FOREWORD

How To Play Hymns And Gospel Songs In Evangelistic Styles, is presented in three sections. The first section presents how to play hymns in Basic Chorale Style. This means that the alto, tenor, and soprano voices of a standard hymn are played by the right hand, and the bass voice is played in octaves by the left hand.

Each hymn used in this section is first presented as it appears in most standard hymnals. The only difference is the addition of chord letter names that appear above the treble staff. In time these chord letter names will enable you to improvise in any style that you choose.

For reference each measure is numbered.

Following the hymn as presented in most standard hymnals, measure by measure examples are given on how to arrange the hymn in Basic Chorale Style. Last, the completely rearranged hymn is given.

To reinforce your knowledge of keyboard harmony, it is recommended that another book, ADVANCED HYMN PLAYING KEYBOARD HARMONY WORKBOOK, Level VII of the DAVID CARR GLOVER Sacred Music Library be used along with this first section.

The second section of How To Play Hymns And Gospel Songs In Evangelistic Styles, presents how to play hymns in Full Chorale and Accompaniment Styles. In Full Chorale Style, the right hand plays the soprano voice in octaves filling in with the tenor and alto. The left hand is the same as in Basic Chorale Style. In Accompaniment Style, the right hand is the same as for Full Chorale Style but one octave higher than written. The left hand plays octaves on the strong beats and chords on the weak beats.

As in the first section of this book, the second section presents the hymn as it appears in most standard hymnals. Chord letter names above the treble staff are given and each measure is numbered for reference.

Measure by measure examples follow on how to arrange the hymn in Full Chorale Style or Accompaniment Style. Last, the completely rearranged hymn is given.

ADVANCED HYMN PLAYING KEYBOARD HARMONY WORKBOOK, Level VIII of the DAVID CARR GLOVER Sacred Music Library is recommended to be used along with this second section.

The third section of How To Play Hymns And Gospel Songs In Evangelistic Styles, is a collection of well loved standard Gospel hymns, already arranged for you, using the three Styles taught in sections one and two. Chord letter names appear above the treble staff for each selection.

This book, How To Play Hymns And Gospel Songs In Evangelistic Styles, is not for the beginner. For the beginner there are books in the DAVID CARR GLOVER Sacred Music Library, Primer and Levels I - VI.

Before beginning this book you should be able to play well many hymns as written in a hymnal. You should also have a basic knowledge and fluent playing technic of chords and their inversions in all keys as well as ALL Major and Minor Scales. To be able to pedal correctly is most important.

Since phrasing and dynamics are not indicated in a hymnal, they are not shown in this book. However, by using the lyrics (words) as a guide, these important fundamentals in hymn interpretation are possible.

To gain facility in playing Gospel music, you should play other hymns in addition to those presented, applying each step as learned. Use any hymnal as the basic principles presented here apply to all hymns and songs written in four part harmony.

The knowledge learned from this book will stimulate your interest in playing hymns correctly and fluently as well as the continued study of other types of Gospel music.

FDL 760

CONTENTS

SECTION ONE

SECTION TWO

SECTION TWO (Cont'd)

SECTION THREE

DAVID CARR GLOVER, 1925-1988

was the creator of the DAVID CARR GLOVER SACRED MUSIC LIBRARY for Piano, the BELWIN ORGAN LIBRARY, THE CONTEMPORARY ORGAN COURSE, and the DAVID CARR GLOVER PIANO LIBRARY as well as a vast amount of other educational keyboard materials.

He was a teacher, composer, editor and lecturer. His lectures and demonstrations included the Walt Disney Studios and the Rose Room in Carnegie Hall. Also he lectured at many Universities and Colleges as well as leading music stores throughout the country.

Mr. Glover was the President-Director of the Glover School of Music for over twenty-five years. The "On Location Workshop" sponsored by his school during the first week of August each year was an event attended by music educators from throughout the United States and Canada.

He was Organ Editor for the School Musician magazine, contributing piano reviewer for the American Music Teacher magazine, founder and President of the Tidewater Music Teachers Forum, and served as consultant and editor for many leading music publishers.

PHYLLIS GUNTHER

currently teaches piano and organ in Wheaton, Illinois. She received her musical training at Wheaton College where she studied with Lester Groom adn Frank Van Deusen, who was the inspiration behind the many Van Deusen Organ Clubs throughout the country.

Mrs. Gunther is a nationally certified member of the Music Teachers National Association, and a member of the National Association of Organ Teachers. She is State Scholarship Foundation Chairman for the Illinois State Music Teachers, after having held numerous positions on the State Governing Board of ISMTA. She is an adjudicator for student auditions in ISMTA, and also for the National Guild of Piano Teachers.

With an extensive background of performance as a soloist and an accompanist, she has also been a partner of a two-piano team for many years. She is an active member of several Music Clubs in her area, performing regularly. She has participated as panelist and speaker for numerous music teachers' workshops and as a clinician, she is extremely well regarded.

Mrs. Gunther has written many arrangements for piano ensemble, published by Belwin-Mills, and is a major contributor to the David Carr Glover Sacred Music Piano Library and the Contemporary Organ Course.

SECTION ONE

How To Play Hymns and Gospel Songs In Evangelistic Styles

Fairest Lord Jesus
(Crusader's Hymn)

As written in a hymnal.

From the German, 17th Century.

Silesian Folk Song (1842)
Arr. by RICHARD S. WILLIS (1819 - 1900)

You are now ready for a new book ADVANCED HYMN PLAYING KEYBOARD HARMONY WORKBOOK LEVEL VII of the DAVID CARR GLOVER SACRED MUSIC LIBRARY for Piano.

FDL 760

How Hymns Are Notated in a Hymnal

Hymns are usually notated (written) in four-part or four-voice harmony. From the lowest to the highest voice, they are called bass, tenor, alto and soprano. The following examples are from the hymn *Fairest Lord Jesus* which is presented on page 4 of this book.

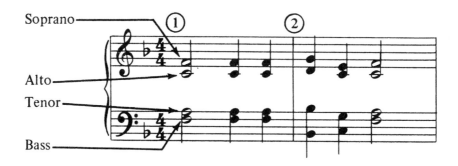

When all four voices of a chord are played or sung together, one complete sound called harmony is the result. It is most helpful when arranging hymns to be able to recognize on the printed page each individual voice and to know the sound of each voice even though they are usually played together.

Play the following voices separately and listen. When you are certain you can recognize each played separately then play all four voices together.

An accomplished performer when playing all four voices can at any time make a single voice stand out above the other three should he so desire.

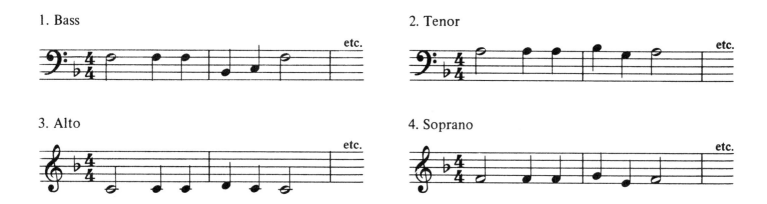

1. Bass

2. Tenor

3. Alto

4. Soprano

All Four Voices Together

When a hymn is played as written in the hymnal, the right hand plays the alto and soprano voices which are notated on the treble staff. The left hand plays the bass and tenor voices which are notated on the bass staff.

Basic Chorale Style
using the hymn
Fairest Lord Jesus

In Basic Chorale Style, the right hand plays the soprano, alto and tenor voices usually on the treble clef staff.

The left hand plays the bass voice almost always on the bass clef staff with the thumb, and adds a tone one octave lower played with the fifth finger.

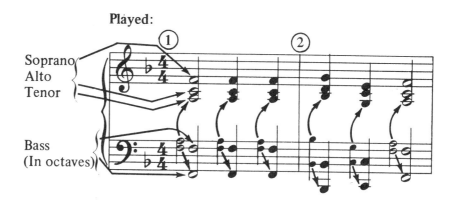

You will note in the above example that though the tenor voice was moved to the right hand it was still played in the same position as given on the staff. However, when the tenor voice is in a position on the staff too far to reach with the right hand, move the tenor up one octave higher placing it on the treble staff between the soprano and alto voices.

Written:

Played:

FDL 760

8

Fairest Lord Jesus, continued

If the original hymn uses the same tone for two voices (soprano and alto or soprano and tenor in octaves), it is usually better to substitute the bass note for the alto or tenor. Keep in mind that the right hand whenever possible plays three different voices of a chord.

Written:

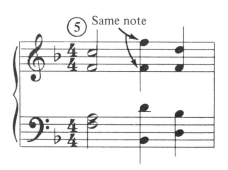

The above is illustrated in measure 5, right hand, third beat, when the alto and soprano use the same note F.

When the tenor note D is moved to the treble clef (Ex. 1), the two F's and the D when sounded together are not as pleasing and are more awkward to play. In Example 2, the alto F is omitted and in its place the Bb is used from the bass. This gives a closer sound, is more in keeping with the chords played before and after, and is easier to play than Example 1

Example 1

Example 2

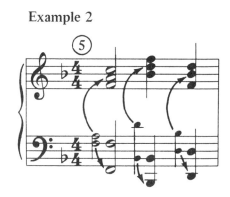

In measure 6, right hand, first two-beat chord, the tenor note A moves to the treble clef. In the next two chords, beats three and four, the tenor half-note C moves to the treble and is changed to two quarter notes.

Written:

Played:

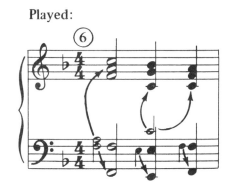

Fairest Lord Jesus, continued

The same basic principles apply in measures 9 and 10 as apply to measures 5 and 6. However, there are two exceptions.

1.   Measure 9 – the first two-beat chord.

Since the tenor note is C, when it is moved to the treble clef (Ex. 1) the two C's along with the alto A when sounded together are not as pleasing and are awkward to play. In Example 2, the tenor C is omitted and in its place the A is used from the bass.

Written:

Example 1

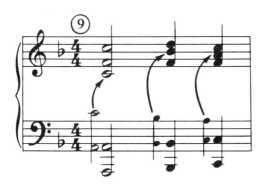

Example 2

2.   Measure 10 – right hand, first two beats.

Instead of playing a single soprano A, second beat, repeat the alto F♯ found on the first beat and add the missing D (bass voice, first beat) to complete the chord. The bass D should also be added to the last chord, beats three and four.

Written:

Played:

Fairest Lord Jesus, continued

In measure 12, right hand, first beat, move the tenor note G to the treble.

Second beat, repeat the alto E and move the bass C to the treble.

Third beat, this chord as written has only two notes, F and A. It is an F Major Chord with the fifth of the chord missing. Fill in this missing C.

Fourth beat, move the tenor C to the treble staff.

Written: **Played:**

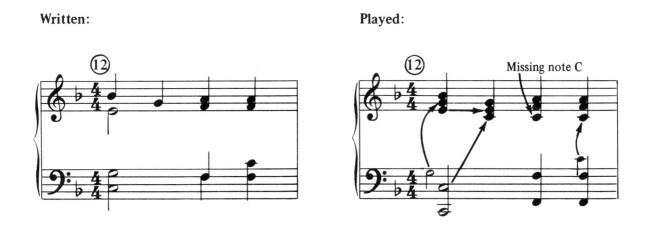

With the principles you now know for playing Basic Chorale Style, fill in the one four-beat chord found in measure 15. This chord is missing a note as shown above in measure 12, third beat.

Written: **Played:**

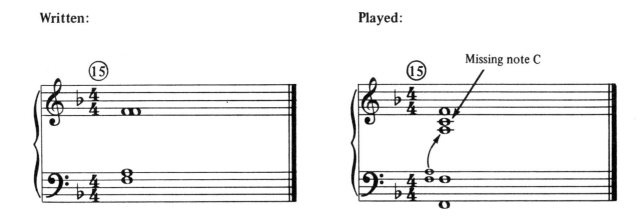

Before playing *Fairest Lord Jesus* in Basic Chorale Style which follows on the next page, thoroughly understand pages 5 through 10.

FDL 760

Fairest Lord Jesus
(Crusader's Hymn)
Basic Chorale Style
(A suggested introduction will be found on page 32.)

Silesian Folk Song

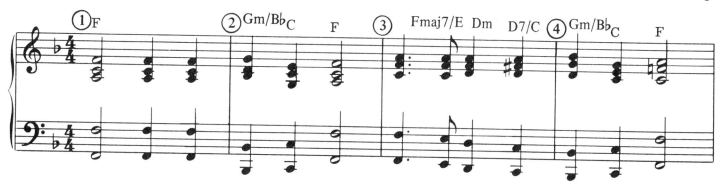

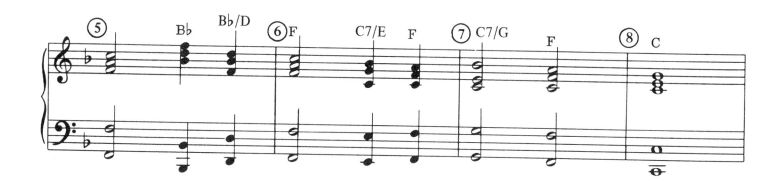

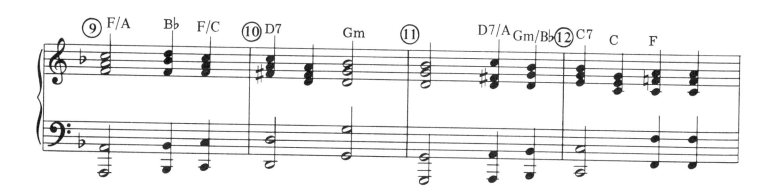

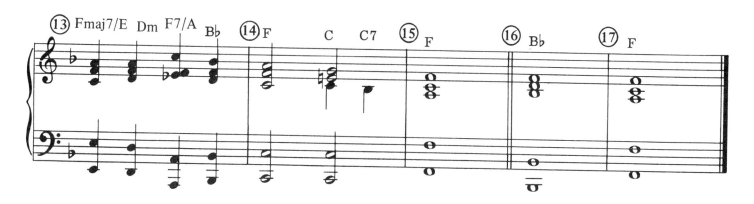

Doxology
(Praise God From Whom All Blessings Flow)

As written in a hymnal.

THOMAS KEN (1637 - 1711)

LOUIS BOURGEOIS (c. 1510 - c. 1561)
Genevan Psalter (1551)

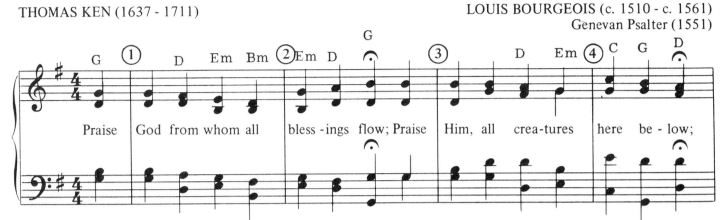

Praise God from whom all bless-ings flow; Praise Him, all crea-tures here be-low;

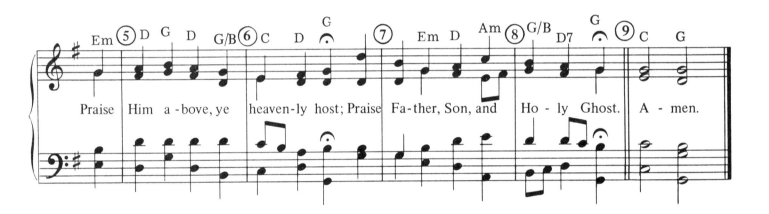

Praise Him a-bove, ye heaven-ly host; Praise Fa-ther, Son, and Ho-ly Ghost. A-men.

To play the *Doxology (Praise God From Whom All Blessings Flow)* in Basic Chorale Style, the right hand again plays the soprano, alto and tenor voices. The left hand plays the bass in octaves.

In measure 2, right hand, it would be best not to move the tenor note G to the treble staff because the soprano uses the same note. As stated earlier in this book, it is better whenever possible to use three different notes in the right hand. With this in mind, the bass note E could be used in the treble, therefore, giving the three different notes desired. For the left hand, the bass note E could still be used played in octaves.

Written:

Played:

FDL 760

Doxology, continued

In measure 3, right hand, first beat, as in measure 2, the soprano and tenor voices use the same note. Substitute the bass note G for the tenor B.

The second and third-beat chords offer no new procedures.

The four-beat chord uses only one note for both soprano and alto voices. In order for the right hand to have three different notes, move both bass and tenor voice notes to the treble staff.

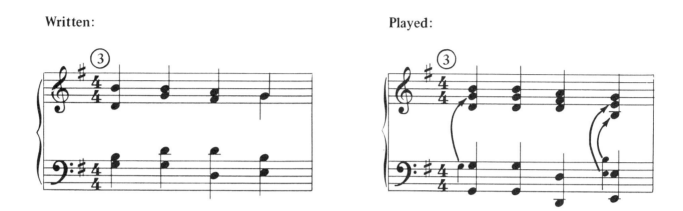

In measure 4, right hand, first beat, fill in the right hand using the same procedures as presented in measure 3, right hand, fourth beat.

In measure 5, right hand, fourth beat, substitute the bass note B for the tenor D since the alto is also D.

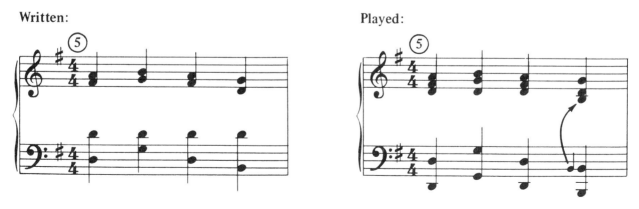

FDL 760

Doxology, continued

In measure 6, right hand, first beat, this chord as written has only two notes—C and E. It is a C Major Chord with the fifth of the chord G omitted. Fill in this missing G.

The second and third-beat chords offer no new procedures.

In the fourth-beat chord, the alto and soprano use the same note D. Omit the alto D and move the bass G and tenor B to complete the three-note right hand chord.

Written:

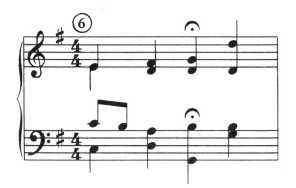

Played:

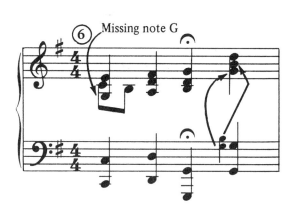

In measure 7, right hand, first beat, for this chord move the tenor G to the treble clef.

The second-beat chord needs to be filled in as shown in measure 4, first beat.

The third-beat chord offers no new procedures.

For the fourth-beat chord, since the alto and tenor voices have the same note E, omit the tenor E and move the bass A to the treble staff.

Written:

Played:

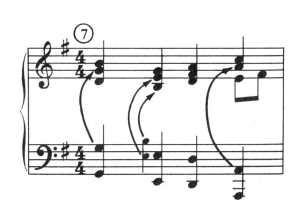

Doxology, continued

In measure 8, right hand, third beat, this chord as written has only two notes—G and B. It is a G Major Chord with the fifth of the chord D missing. Fill in this missing D.

Written: Played:

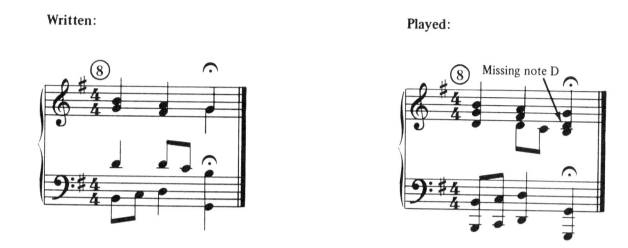

You are ready to play the Doxology in Basic Chorale Style.

Doxology
(Praise God From Whom All Blessings Flow)

(A suggested introduction will be found on page 32.)

THOMAS KEN   LOUIS BOURGEOIS

FDL 760

When Morning Gilds The Skies
(Laudes Domini)

As written in a hymnal.

From the German (19th Century)
Tr. by EDWARD CASWELL (1814 - 1878)

JOSEPH BARNBY (1838 - 1896)

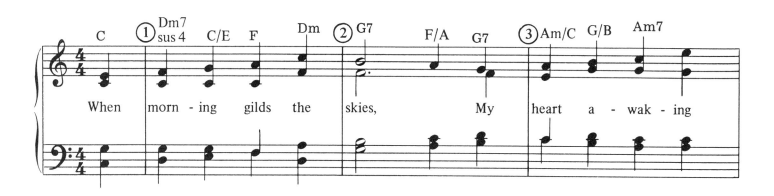

When morn - ing gilds the skies, My heart a - wak - ing

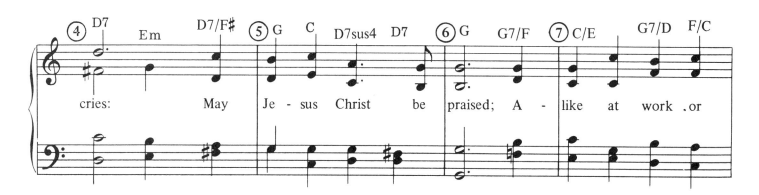

cries: May Je - sus Christ be praised; A - like at work .or

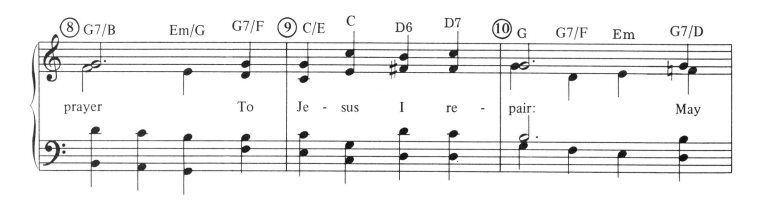

prayer To Je - sus I re - pair: May

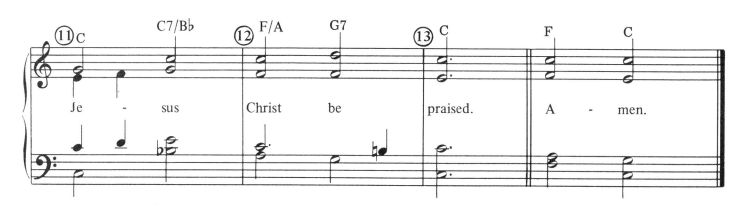

Je - sus Christ be praised. A - men.

FDL 760

When Morning Gilds The Skies, continued

In measure 1, right hand, second beat, the tenor and soprano use the same note G. Omit the tenor G and move bass E to the treble. All other chords in this measure present no new procedures.

In measure 2, right hand, third beat, repeat the alto note F and bring the tenor note C to the treble.

In measure 3, right hand, third beat, the tenor and soprano voices use the same note C. Omit the tenor C and move the bass A to the treble.

All other chords in measures 3 and 4 present no new procedures.

Written:

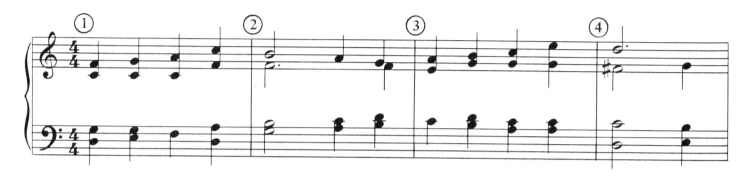

Played:

In measure 5, right hand, first half of the fourth beat, move up the bass D, 2nd tenor F♯, repeat the alto C, and sustain the soprano A for its dotted quarter note value.

Written: Played:

For simplicity you may wish to play only the soprano note.

FDL 760

When Morning Gilds The Skies, continued

In measure 7, all of the procedures for arranging this in the Basic Chorale Style have been presented in previous examples. However, for reinforcement the procedures are given again.

In the first-beat chord, the alto and tenor have the same note C. Omit the tenor C and move up the bass E.

In the second-beat chord, the soprano and alto have the same note C. Omit the alto C and move up the tenor G and the bass E.

In the third-beat chord, the soprano and tenor have the same note B. Omit the tenor B and move up the bass D.

In the fourth-beat chord, move up the tenor A.

Written: Played:

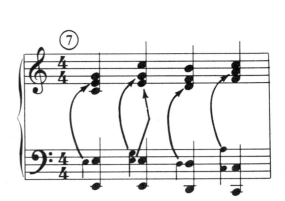

In measure 9, again the procedures are presented for reinforcement.

In the first-beat chord, the tenor and alto have the same note C. Omit the tenor C and move up the bass E.

In the second-beat chord, bring up the tenor G.

In the third-beat chord, bring up the tenor D.

In the fourth-beat chord, the soprano and tenor have the same note C. Omit the tenor C and move up the bass D.

Written: Played:

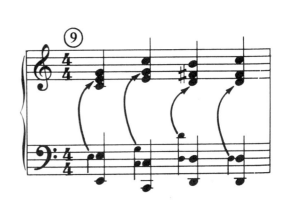

When Morning Gilds The Skies
Basic Chorale Style
(A suggested introduction will be found on page 32.)

From the German
Tr. by EDWARD CASWALL

JOSEPH BARNBY

All Hail The Power
(Coronation)

As written in a hymnal.

EDWARD PERRONET (1726 - 1792)
JOHN RIPPON (1751 - 1836)

OLIVER HOLDEN (1765 - 1844)

Play this hymn in Basic Chorale Style filling in the necessary chords and rearranging the bass.

FDL 760

All Hail The Power, continued

Now you should be ready to go on to the next step in playing chorale style. The left hand acts as a basic beat. If there is a half note in the bass, instead of holding it for two beats, the left hand plays an octave followed by a chord. The octave and the chord would each have the time value of a quarter note. If there is a dotted half note in the bass, the left hand plays an octave and two chords. Similarly, if there is a whole note, the left hand plays an octave followed by three chords. Be careful to play the identical chord notes in the left hand as are found in the right hand. However, any position of the chord may be used.

See measures 4, 7, 9, 12, 14 and 15.

Positions of the chord (Triad)

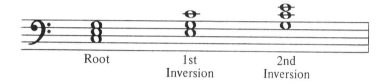

Root   1st Inversion   2nd Inversion

Written: **Played:** Same note (different octaves)

In the given example, the left hand chord position though an octave lower is the same as the right hand. This is preferred when possible.

At the end of a hymn use the first inversion of the chord as the last chord in the left hand. This along with the sound of the octave root bass, usually played on the first beat of the measure and sustained with the damper pedal, gives a sound of completeness that is desired.

Written: **Played:**

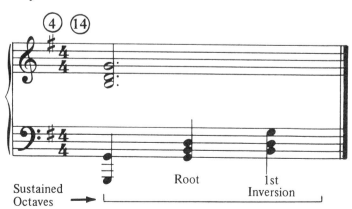

Sustained Octaves   Root   1st Inversion

All Hail The Power, continued

In measure 8, the principle is the same as the one found in measure 7. On the second and fourth beats, the chord position though an octave lower is the same as the right hand.

Written: Played:

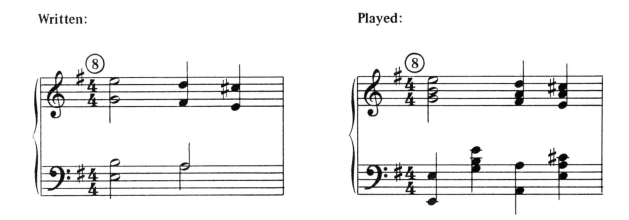

Another principle to follow is when the right hand has a dotted quarter note followed by an eighth note, the left hand plays in quarter note rhythm.

In measure 13, the above is found.

Written: Played:

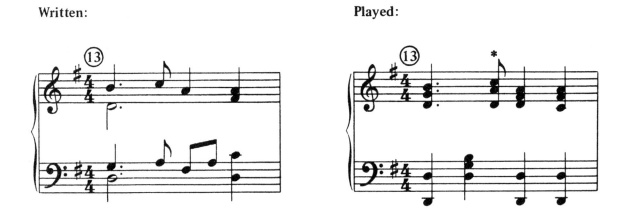

*For simplicity you may wish to play only the soprano note C.

All Hail The Power

Basic Chorale Style

From the examples of introductions presented on page 32, you should be able to decide upon a suitable introduction for this hymn and others presented in this book.

EDWARD PERRONET
JOHN RIPPON

OLIVER HOLDEN

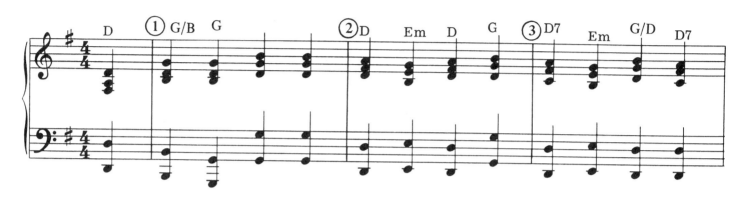

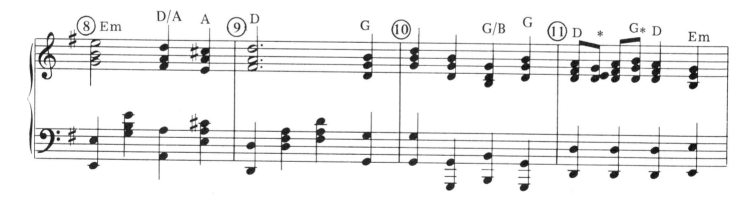

For simplicity, play soprano note only.

FDL 760

Come, Thou Almighty King
(Italian Hymn)

As written in a hymnal.

Author unknown

FELICE de GIARDINI (1716 - 1796)

Come, Thou Almighty King, continued

Play *Come, Thou Almighty King* in Basic Chorale Style filling in the chords of the right hand whenever necessary. In measure 3, 6, 8, 16, 17 and 18, left hand, play an octave followed by two chords instead of the dotted half notes as written.

Written: Played:

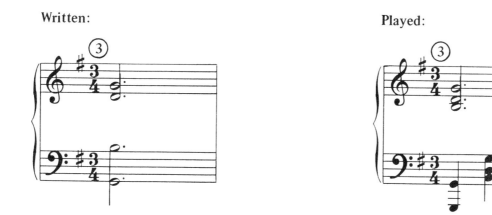

In measures 7, 8 and 13, right hand, play single notes as written rather than filling in with chords. For the left hand use octaves. Other hymns have similar passages which are far more effective if not filled in with chords. This lends variety and a dramatic quality to your performance.

Written: Played:

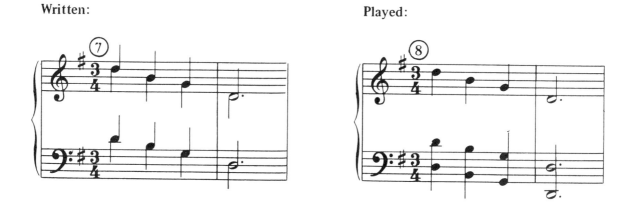

Come, Thou Almighty King, continued

In measures 9 and 10, left hand, also measures 11 and 12, the bass has repeated D's and G's. You may wish to change this bass to make it more interesting. Another note from the alto and tenor could be used. Sometimes the composer of the original hymn has left out a note that belongs to the chord. Such a note could be added which also makes the bass more interesting.

In measure 9, the third-beat chord is a D7. The note of F♯ is not given. This note could be used for the bass.

Written:

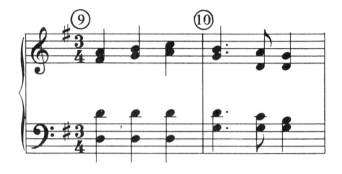

Played:

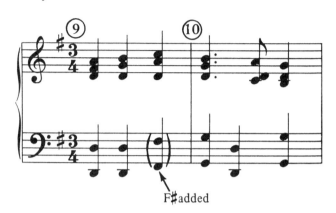

F♯added

Contrary Motion

Contrary Motion in music means when the parts are moving in opposite directions. Whenever possible it is wise to consider contrary motion. It usually makes the music sound more interesting. An example of contrary motion is if the soprano voice moves up the bass voice moves down or just the opposite. You should experiment with several ways whenever possible.

In the example above, measure 10 is presented with contrary motion. In the following example, measures 9 and 10, beginning with the third beat of measure 9, another form of contrary motion is given.

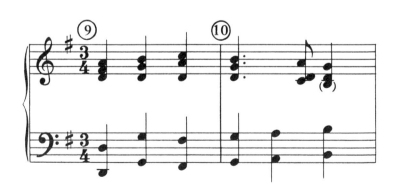

Come, Thou Almighty King
Basic Chorale Style

From the examples of introductions presented on page 32, you should be able to decide upon a suitable introduction for this hymn and others presented in this book.

Author unknown

FELICE de GIARDINI

FDL 760

How Firm A Foundation
(Portuguese Hymn) or (Adeste Fideles)

As written in a hymnal.

"K" in Rippon's
"Selection of Hymns" (1787)

J. F. WADE'S
Cantus Diversi (1751)

Chords

All chords in root position are built in thirds, stacked on top of each other. The simplest chord is the triad which has three notes. When a chord has more than three notes, a number HIGHER THAN 5 is placed after the letter name. The following examples of chords that have numbers after them higher than 5 are based on the degrees of the C Major Scale and by no means are intended to be complete. It should, however, help in the analysis of chords presented in this library. They may be transposed into all other keys based on a major scale.

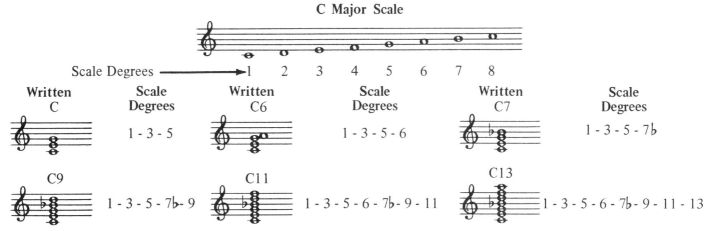

In chords some notes are more important than others. Should a note be omitted, leave out the least important. Whenever possible the root and third should be used and the note represented by the number next to the chord letter name. For 9th, 11th and 13th chords when given the 7th should, if possible, be included also.

The Seventh Chord

Seventh chords have four different notes. When they are given in Basic Chorale Style, use all four notes in the right hand rather than three. There are several kinds of seventh chords. Below are three of them based on the degrees of the C Major Scale. However, the same rule applies to all other keys.

Quality	Scale Degrees	Note Names	Written
Dominant Seventh	1 - 3 - 5 - 7♭	C - E - G - B♭	C7
Minor Seventh	1 - 3♭- 5 - 7♭	C - E♭- G - B♭	Cm7
Major Seventh	1 - 3 - 5 - 7	C - E - G - B	Cmaj.7

How Firm A Foundation, continued

On the following pages will be found *How Firm A Foundation* presented in Basic Chorale Style. Fill in the right hand with chords and the left hand half and dotted half notes with octaves and chords.

In measure 4, fourth beat, and measure 5, first beat, will be found Dominant Seventh Chords.

Written: **Played:**

Seventh Chords will also be found in measures 6, 7, 9, 10, 15, 17, 18 and 19.

How Firm A Foundation, continued

To make the bass more interesting, in measures 9, 10 and 11, study the example below. Use tenor notes instead of some of the bass notes. On the first beat of measure 9, right hand, play an octave with the chord filled in. Notes in parentheses indicate bass line to be used.

On the last beat of measure 12, all of measure 13, and the last three beats of measure 14, right hand, use single notes rather than filling in the chords. In the left hand use octaves. In measure 12, left hand, it sounds better to rest on the third beat.

Play single note F (soprano) if desired.

How Firm A Foundation
Basic Chorale Style

From the examples of introductions presented on page 32. you should be able to decide upon a suitable introduction for this hymn and others presented in this book.

"K" in Rippon's
"Selection of Hymns"

J. F. WADE'S
Cantus Diversi

*Play single soprano note if desired.

FDL 760

Introductions

It is customary in some churches for the accompanist to play through the entire hymn as an introduction. However, when a shorter introduction is desired, the accompanist should be careful in choosing one. It is usually best to play the last phrase or the last two phrases of a hymn for this purpose. Other ways are also possible. The words should be your guide. When the phrase begins on an incomplete measure, be sure to include these notes instead of beginning on the first beat of a measure. The *Doxology* and *When Morning Gilds The Skies* are both examples of introductions beginning on an incomplete measure. They are presented below.

Examples For Introductions
Fairest Lord Jesus

To be found on page 11.

Doxology
(Praise God From Whom All Blessings Flow)

To be found on page 15.

When Morning Gilds The Skies

To be found on page 19.

SECTION TWO

How To Play Hymns and Gospel Songs In Evangelistic Styles

Review

Before beginning this section, let us review the principles presented in SECTION ONE.

1. In Basic Chorale Style double the bass note in the left hand in octaves. Play the tenor, alto and soprano notes with the right hand. Fill in the missing notes of the chord in the right hand whenever necessary.

Written: Played:

2. When there are half notes, dotted half notes and whole notes in the left hand after playing the octave, fill in the remaining beats with chords keeping the left hand moving at all times. Be careful to play identical chord notes in the left hand as found in the right hand.

Written: Played:

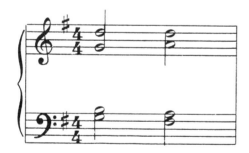 

Same notes as in right hand.

3. When the right hand has a dotted quarter note followed by an eighth note, the left hand plays quarter notes. In the above example and the one below, the left hand chord position though an octave lower is the same as the right hand. This is preferred when possible, however, any position of the chord may be used.

Written: Played:

For simplicity you can play only the soprano note C.

Review, continued

4.   At the end of a hymn use the first inversion of the chord as the last chord in the left hand. This along with the sound of the octave root base, usually played on the first beat of the measure and sustained with the damper pedal, gives a sound of completeness that is desired.

<table>
<tr><td>Written:</td><td>Played:</td></tr>
</table>

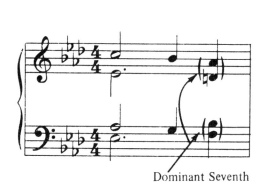 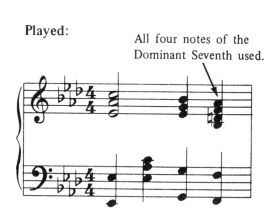

5.   Always play four notes of a Seventh Chord.

Written: Played:

All four notes of the
Dominant Seventh used.

Dominant Seventh

6.   When there are repeated bass notes, you may wish to find a more interesting left hand to play. Use tenor or alto notes in addition to the bass. Experiment until you find what you like. There could be more than one way, and you do not have to play a hymn exactly the same way twice.

Written: Played:

7.   Remember to look carefully at the key and time signatures. Choose your introduction and practice each hymn with an introduction included. Play with a firm touch, bring out the melody, keep a steady beat, and do not drag the tempo. Most important, you lead the congregation; and above all pedal correctly.

You are now ready for the first hymn to be presented in Full Chorale Style — *All Hail The Power.*

All Hail The Power
(Coronation)

As written in a hymnal.

EDWARD PERRONET (1726 - 1792)
JOHN RIPPON (1751 - 1836)

OLIVER HOLDEN (1765 - 1844)

Chord letter names enclosed in parentheses are to be considered secondary in importance and could be omitted.

The 6th Chord

When a 6 is placed after a chord letter name it means an interval of a second has been added to a Triad. When the triad used is major or minor and in root position, the second added on top to form the 6th chord is a major second (one whole step). Like all chords the 6th chord can be inverted.

When you become experienced in arranging hymns, you may wish to add a 6th tone to a major or minor triad. Such chords should be used seldom; and if in doubt, not at all.

The 6th chord was also presented on page 29, SECTION ONE of this book.

You are now ready for a new book ADVANCED HYMN PLAYING KEYBOARD HARMONY WORKBOOK, Level VIII of the DAVID CARR GLOVER SACRED MUSIC LIBRARY for Piano.

All Hail The Power, continued

Full Chorale Style

In Full Chorale Style the right hand plays the soprano voice in octaves with the tenor and alto voices filling in between. The left hand is played the same way as in Basic Chorale Style.

Written:

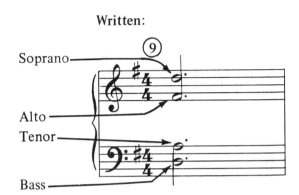

Played:

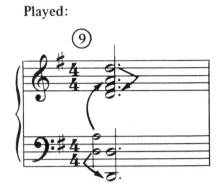

When the right hand plays half and dotted half notes as well as sustained tones, the left hand plays an octave followed by a single bass note. If possible the single bass note should be played one octave lower than the bottom of the octave. Also other notes within the chord may be used for the single bass note. Your ear and good taste should be your guide.

Written:

Played:

In measure 8, left hand, third and fourth beats, two octaves may be played rather than an octave followed by a single note.

Written:

Played:

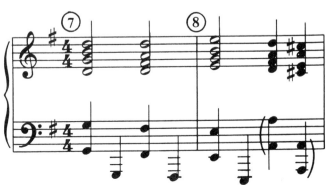

All Hail The Power, continued

In Full Chorale Style when a seventh chord is used in the right hand, you may wish to leave out the lower note of the octave which is the soprano that has been doubled. If not, you would be playing five notes that could be awkward and too thick in sound. The four remaining notes should include the seventh tone of the chord. If the root of the chord is not in the left hand, it too should be included in the right hand. The following examples present chords with four and five notes. Seventh chords are found in measure 3.

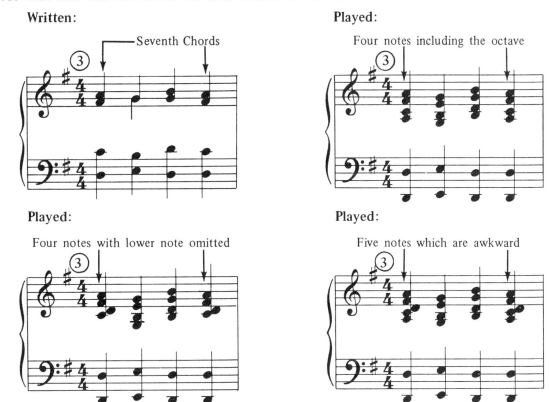

In measure 11, left hand, second beat, you may play an octave on F♯ rather than repeat the bass note D for three beats. This gives a more interesting bass.

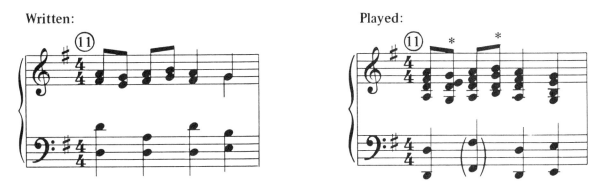

In measure 13, the left hand plays quarter notes throughout the measure. On the third beat the right hand plays a chord in quarter notes rather than playing the eighth notes found in the tenor (bass clef).

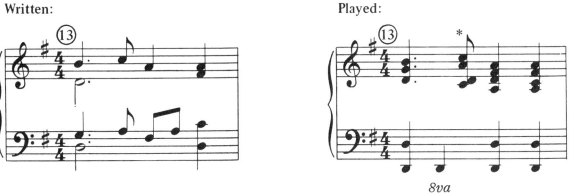

8va

For simplicity, octaves may be used without the full chord.

All Hail The Power
Full Chorale Style

EDWARD PERRONET
JOHN RIPPON

OLIVER HOLDEN

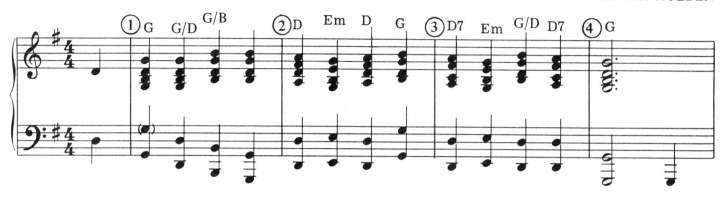

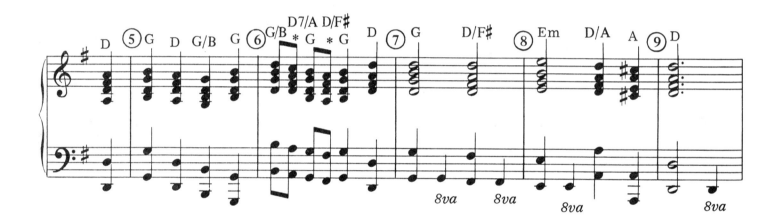

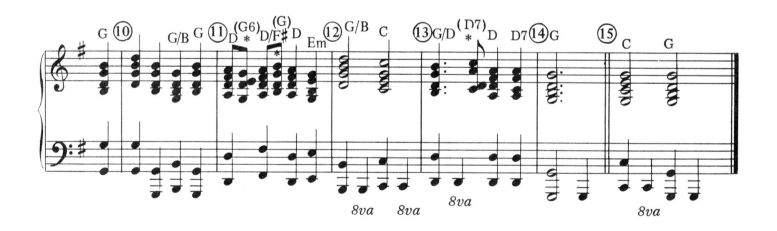

For simplicity, octaves may be used without the full chord. You will also note that some chord letter names are enclosed with parentheses. This is because they are secondary in importance and could be omitted.

FDL 760

O God, Our Help In Ages Past

(St. Anne)

As written in a hymnal.

From Psalm 90
ISSAC WATTS (1674 - 1748)

WILLIAM CROFT (1678 - 1727)

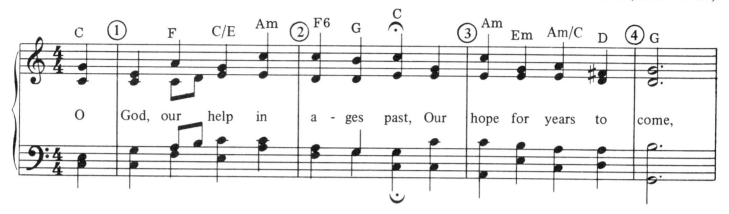

O God, our help in a - ges past, Our hope for years to come,

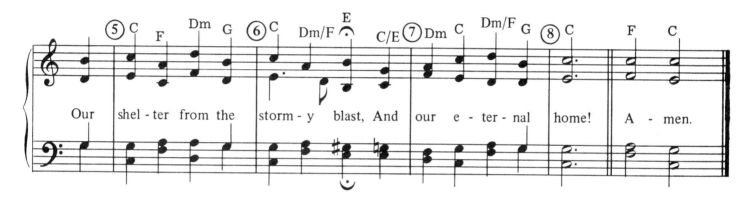

Our shel - ter from the storm - y blast, And our e - ter - nal home! A - men.

The following procedures are also for playing in Full Chorale Style.

In measure 1, right hand, second beat, play the two top notes together as quarter notes and the two lower notes on each half of the beat in eighth notes.

Written: **Played:**

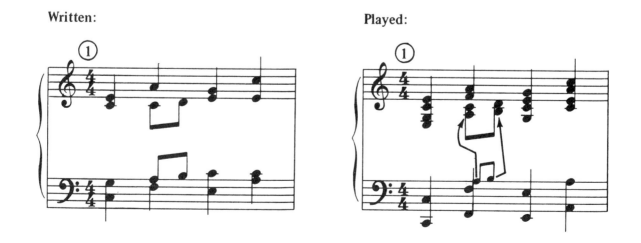

FDL 760

O God, Our Help, continued

In measures 2 and 6, both hands, third beat, will be found a Fermata ($\frown$). If it is observed with a pause, the left hand plays an octave followed by a single note. This will help fill in the pause.

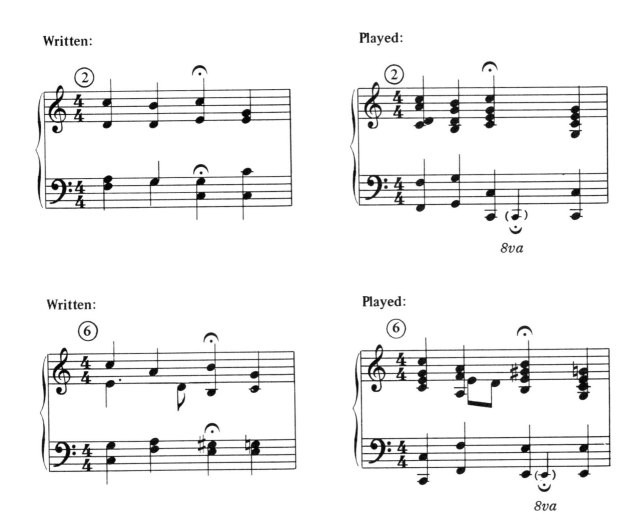

In measures 4 and 8, left hand, as above, a similar bass is used. On beats one and two play an octave followed by a single bass note on beat three.

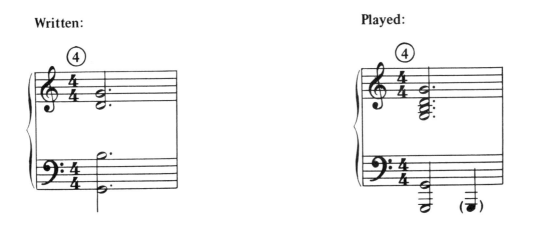

O God, Our Help In Ages Past

Full Chorale Style

From Psalm 90
ISSAC WATTS

WILLIAM CROFT

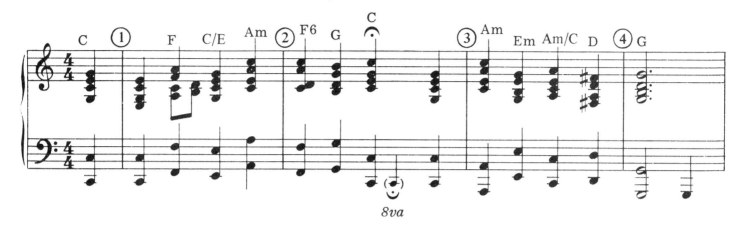

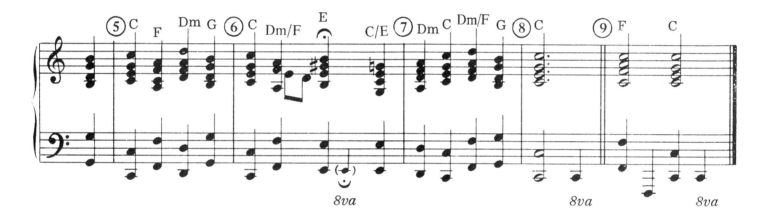

When you have completed O Worship The King on page 42 play other hymns in Full Choral Style. Review all of the hymns presented in SECTION ONE using the Full Chorale Style rather than the Basic Chorale Style. For further reinforcement you may wish to play many hymns from a hymnal.

When you are able to play hymns fluently in Full Chorale Style, you will be ready to proceed to the next step in hymn playing — Accompaniment Style.

Both Basic and Full Chorale Styles are used for worship hymns. Accompaniment Style is used for hymns with moving melodies. The time signatures for these hymns are usually in $\frac{3}{4}$, $\frac{4}{4}$, and $\frac{6}{8}$.

FDL 760

Play the following hymn in Full Chorale Style using the principles learned.

O Worship The King

(Lyons)

As written in a hymnal.

From Psalm 104
ROBERT GRANT (c.1779 - 1838)

J. MICHAEL HAYDN (1737 - 1806)

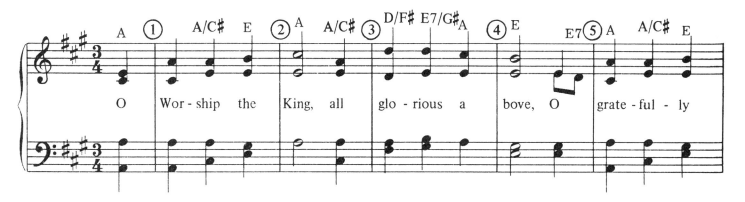

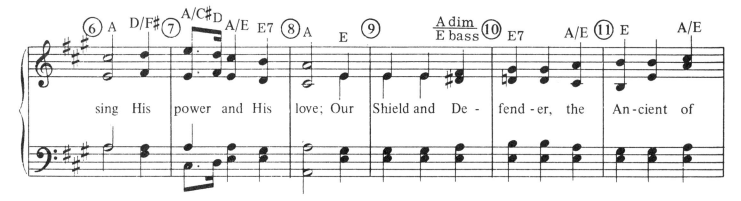

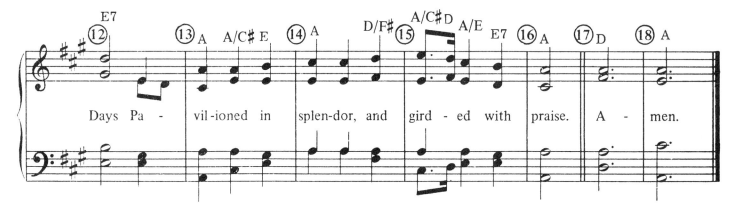

ACCOMPANIMENT STYLE

The right hand will be the same as for Full Chorale but *one octave higher than written.*

For the most part the left hand will play octaves on the strong beats and chords on the weak beats. **Octaves should be used in the left hand when the harmony changes within the measure.**

If the right hand has a dotted note, the left hand does not play the dotted rhythm but keeps a steady beat. This was also done in Basic and Full Chorale Style.

When there are rests in the left hand, rather than having a pause in the accompaniment it is usually best to fill in with octaves and chords.

Faith Of Our Fathers
(St. Catherine)

As written in a hymnal.

FREDERICK W. FABER (1814 - 1863)

HENRI F. HEMY (1818 - 1888)

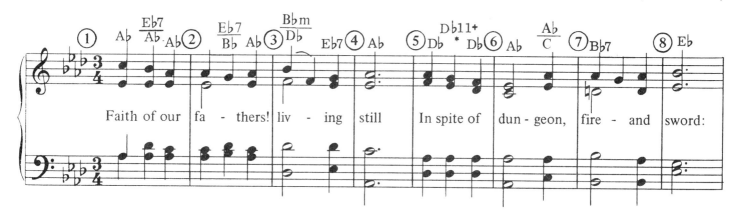

Faith of our fa - thers! liv - ing still In spite of dun - geon, fire - and sword:

O how our hearts beat high — with joy when-e'er we hear that glo - rious word!

Faith of our fa - thers ho - ly faith! We will be true to Thee till death! A - men.

The + sign in measures 5 and 13 (Db 11+) means the eleventh note of the chord Gb has been raised one half step to G.

*The 9th, 11th, and 13th Chords

The following chords are constructed on the C Dominant Seventh Chord in root position.

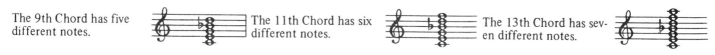

The 9th Chord has five different notes.   The 11th Chord has six different notes.   The 13th Chord has seven different notes.

From the chord examples above you will notice that there are more than four different notes for each. Because of this it is awkward, and usually not necessary, to include all of the notes when such chords are used. For more information on such chords, see page 29, SECTION ONE of this book.

FDL 760

44

Faith Of Our Fathers, continued

This hymn will be presented in Accompaniment Style. The right hand chords are formed the same way as for Full Chorale Style playing except that they are played one octave higher than written. This gives a much fuller sound which is needed in leading a congregation. Also it allows the left hand to move more freely.

In measure 1, left hand, rather than repeat the bass note A♭ in octaves, play an octave on the first beat followed by two chords.

Written:    **Played:**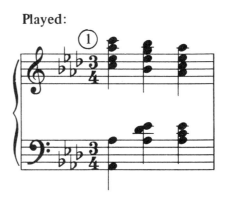

Measures 9 and 21 may also be played as above.

In measure 5, left hand, play an octave followed by two chords.

In measure 6, left hand, play an octave followed by a chord and then another octave.

Written: **Played:**

Here is another way to play measures 5 and 6 which you may find sounds better.

In measure 5, left hand, use the alto notes rather than the bass note D♭ .

In measure 6, left hand, continue to use the alto note of C on the first beat followed by two chords on the second and third beats.

FDL 760

Faith Of Our Fathers, continued

When playing in either Full Chorale or Accompaniment Style, both of which are better when octaves are used for the right hand melody, chords may occur that have four or more different notes. With so many different notes the chord could be awkward or impossible to play. In such an event leave out one or more of the notes between the octave or the lower note of the octave. Should the chord be a Dominant Seventh it is best not to omit the 7th of the chord.

In measure 5 below, the Db 11+ chord is used on the second beat. Only the notes of Db and Eb have been included between the G octave.

You will notice however, that when the Bb 9 chord in measure 15, second beat, right hand is given on page 46, it is possible to use all five different notes. Only the lower note of the C octave is omitted.

In measure 13, left hand, again use the alto voice rather than the bass.

In measure 14, left hand, use the alto voice on the first beat followed by a chord on the second beat and an octave on the third beat.

Written: Played:

Measure 22 should be played in a similar way as measure 14.

In measure 17, left hand, play an octave followed by two chords.

Written: Played:

Faith Of Our Fathers
Accompaniment Style

FREDERICK W. FABER

HENRI F. HEMY

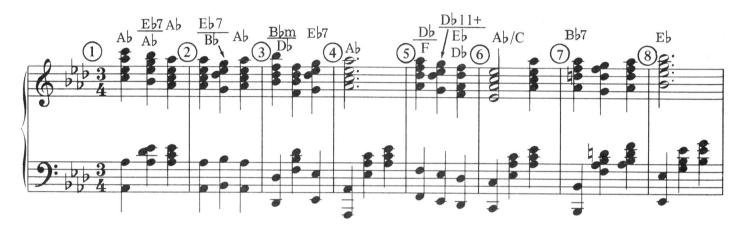

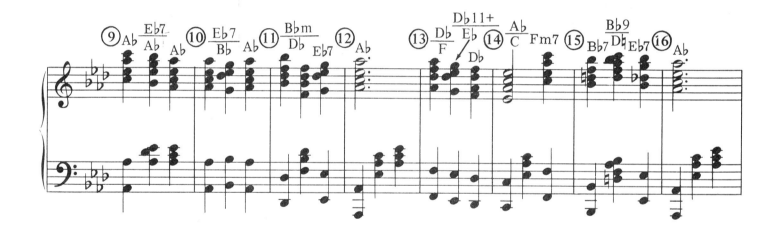

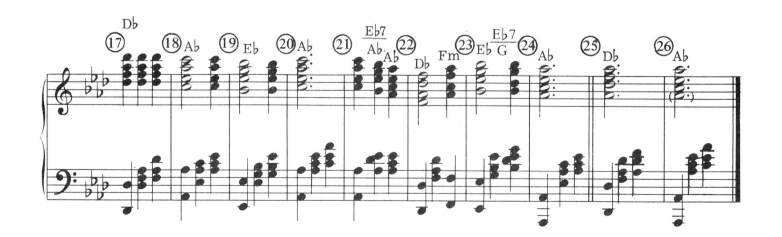

Majestic Sweetness Sits Enthroned

(Ortonville)

As written in a hymnal.

SAMUEL STENNETT (1727 - 1795)   THOMAS HASTINGS (1784 - 1872)

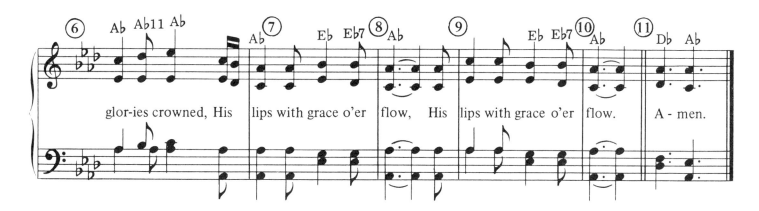

Majestic Sweetness Sits Enthroned, continued

For this hymn with a time signature of six-eight, the left hand plays octaves on the strong beats (one and four) of each measure. On the other beats chords are used. When there is a chord change (new chord) within the measure, the left hand plays an octave (usually the root of the new chord) on the beat.

In measure 1, left hand, octaves are used on beats one and four. Chords are used on the other beats.

In measure 2, left hand, an octave is used on the third beat as well as beats one and four because of the chord change. Note that each of these octaves is the root of the chord.

Written: **Played:**

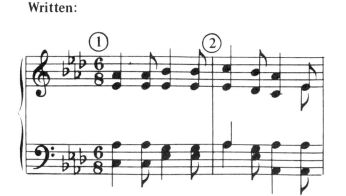

FDL 760

When there is only one chord used in a measure, the harmonies are the same. For variety and interest the following is suggested:

In measure 3, left hand, fourth beat, it is more interesting to play an octave F instead of repeating the bass note D♭ . Also for interest play an octave on the sixth beat.

Written:

Played:

In measures 4, 8 and 10, left hand, where there are dotted quarter notes tied to quarter notes or dotted quarter notes, play an octave on the first beat and then play chords through the fifth beat followed by an octave on the sixth beat, except in measure 10. In this measure the octave is omitted on the sixth beat because the measure is an incomplete last measure with only five beats.

In measure 4, sixth beat, left hand, for variety play an octave on E♭ instead of repeating the bass note A♭ .

Written:

Played:

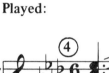

In measure 8, left hand, for variety on the sixth beat play an octave on C instead of repeating the bass note A

Written:

Played:

In measure 6, the left hand plays the tenor notes in octaves on beats three and four. On the sixth beat the left hand matches the right hand rhythm using 16th note octaves. The 16th note octaves played by the left hand are A♭ and B♭ going to an octave C on the first beat in measure 4.

Written:

Played:

Contrary Motion

In measure 6, right hand, sixth beat, the octaves of the chords descend from C to B♭ going to A♭ in the next measure.

In the same measure, left hand, sixth beat, the octaves used ascend from A♭ to B♭ going to C in the next measure.

When both hands of the above are played together, it is a form of playing called Contrary Motion. (See page 26, SECTION ONE of this book.) To most listeners this sounds better than if both hands are moving in the same direction. Contrary motion should be used when possible.

In measure 9, left hand, first beat, you may play the A♭ octave one octave lower than where it would normally fall.

Written: **Played:**

Majestic Sweetness Sits Enthroned
Accompaniment Style

SAMUEL STENNETT

THOMAS HASTINGS

For simplicity, octaves may be used without the full chord.

FDL 760

Saviour, Like A Shepherd Lead Us

As written in a hymnal.

From "Hymns to the Young" (1836)
DOROTHY ANN THRUPP (1779 - 1847)

WILLIAM B. BRADBURY (1816 - 1868)

See page 43 for information on the 9th, 11th and 13th chords.

FDL 760

Saviour, Like A Shepherd Lead Us, continued

Because this hymn is usually sung slowly, the left hand could play the bass in eighth notes instead of quarters using a combination of octaves and chords. When there is a change in harmony an octave is generally used. Since the accompaniment can be played in various ways, the following suggestions are for you to consider.

Measures 1 and 5 are alike. On the first and second beats of the left hand, it sounds better to play an octave and three chords instead of one octave again on the second beat.

Written: **Played:**

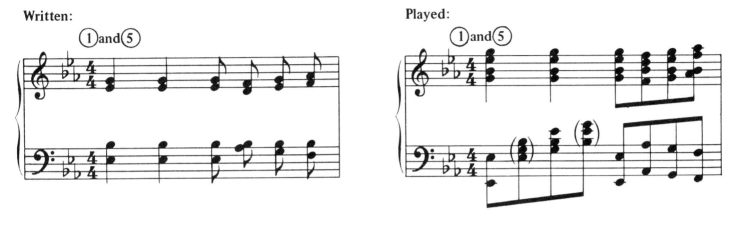

Passing Tones

A note that is not a part of the harmony but is used to fill in and make a passage more interesting is referred to as a Passing Note or Tone.

Written:

Measures 2 and 6 are also alike. Here are two ways in which the left hand can be played using passing tones in octaves.

1. **Played:**

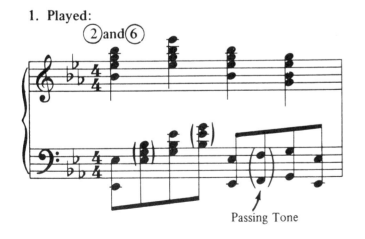

Passing Tone

2. **Played:**

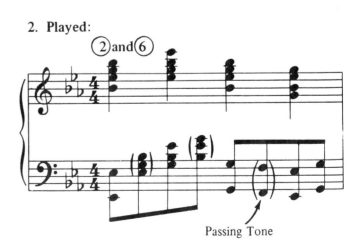

Passing Tone

*For simplicity the chords in parentheses may be omitted. Similar chords throughout this hymn may also be omitted.

Saviour, Like A Shepherd Lead Us, continued

In measures 3 and 7, left hand, change the repeated B♭ octaves. Two ways in which this can be done are shown below.

Written:

1. **Played:**

2. **Played**

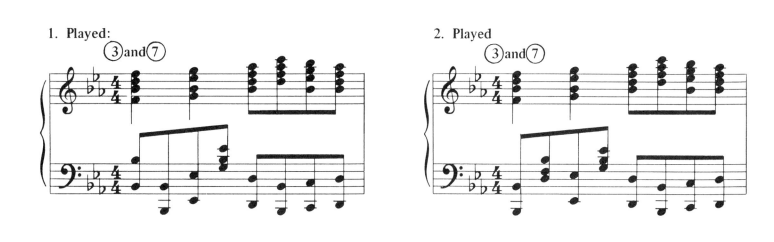

In measure 4, fourth beat, left hand, in place of the rest continue the inversions of the E♭ chord in eighth notes. The right hand also uses an inversion of the E♭ chord; this time, however, in quarter notes.

Written: **Played:**

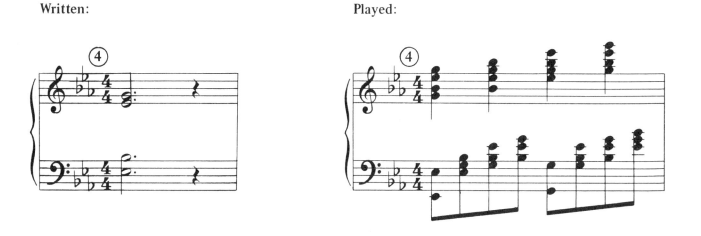

Saviour, Like A Shepherd Lead Us, continued

Measures 8 and 12 are alike. Play them in a similar way to measure 4 filling in the right hand in chords. Here are two examples of what can be done.

Written:

1. Played:

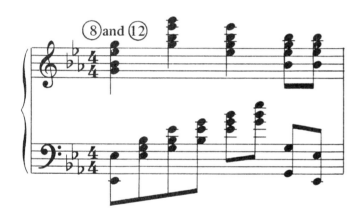

2. Played:

Measures 9 and 13 are also alike. Change the repeated A♭ in the bass. A passing tone sounds good here.

Written:

Played:

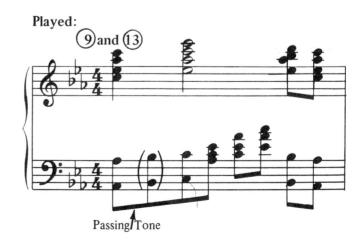

Passing Tone

Saviour, Like A Shepherd Lead Us, continued

In measure 10, left hand, change the repeated E♭. Since the left hand ended on an A♭ octave in measure 9, it sounds best to continue to G (first beat) and go down to E♭ (second beat) in octaves. See example.

Written:

Played:

Passing Tone

In measure 11, left hand, change the repeated B♭ octaves of the bass using chords and passing tones.

Written:

Played:

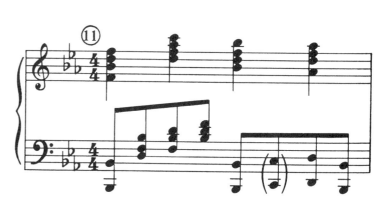

Passing Tone

Saviour, Like A Shepherd Lead Us, continued

Play measure 14 in a similar way to measure 10 except for the fourth beat. Use octaves in both hands for a nice contrary motion sound.

Measure 15, left hand, use a passing tone played in octaves.

Measure 16, fourth beat, both hands sound better if the quarter rest is observed. On the first two beats of the right hand play a half note chord followed by a quarter note chord on the third beat.

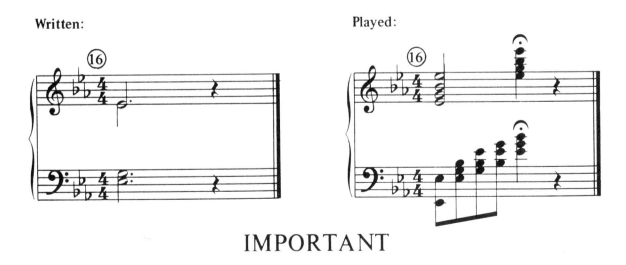

IMPORTANT

Saviour, Like A Shepherd Lead Us like other hymns in this book can be arranged in other ways than those suggested. Experiment with the knowledge you have gained before making a choice. Also remember that you can play any hymn several ways and still be correct. You may wish when playing a hymn for the congregation to play each new stanza with variations. This will add interest and variety to your performance. Remember that only a gifted few can play and arrange a hymn on the first attempt. For most it requires practice and patience.

Saviour, Like A Shepherd Lead Us
Accompaniment Style

DOROTHY ANN THRUPP

WILLIAM B. BRADBURY

By now you should be able to arrange the hymn *What A Friend We Have In Jesus* without further instruction. Play it in accompaniment style using eighth notes in the left hand and other principles taught in the last hymn, *Saviour, Like A Shepherd Lead Us.*

Experiment until you find what you like.

What A Friend We Have In Jesus

As written in a hymnal:

JOSEPH SCRIVEN (1819 - 1886)   CHARLES C. CONVERSE (1832 - 1918)

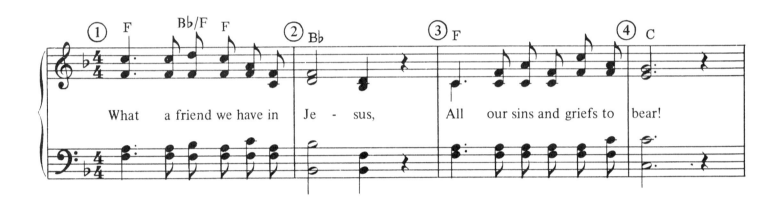

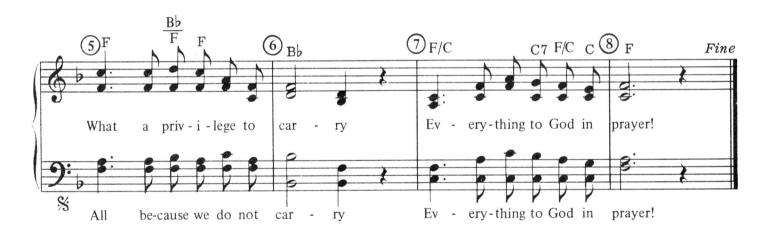

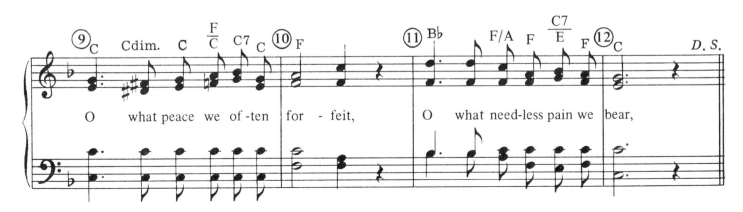

Here is a suggested way to play this hymn. How did your arrangement compare with this? You do not have to play this hymn in exactly the same way presented here. This is only one of several ways.

What A Friend We Have In Jesus
Accompaniment Style

JOSEPH SCRIVEN

CHARLES C. CONVERSE

FDL 760

Play the following hymn in Accompaniment Style using the principles learned.

Onward Christian Soldiers
(St. Gertrude)

As written in a hymnal.

SABINE BARING-GOULD (1834 - 1924)　　　　　ARTHUR SULLIVAN (1842 - 1900)

Here is one way to play this hymn. How did your arrangement compare with this?

Onward Christian Soldiers
(Accompaniment Style)

Traditional

SUMMARY

1. Look carefully at the key and time signatures. Choose your introductions carefully and practice each hymn with an introduction included. Play with a firm touch and a steady rhythm, bringing out the melody at all times.

2. Usually play all worship hymns in Basic or Full Chorale Styles.

3. In Basic Chorale Style, the right hand plays the soprano, tenor, and alto. The left hand plays the bass in octaves. In Full Chorale style, for the most part, the right hand plays the soprano and the note one octave below, filling in with the tenor and alto. The left hand is the same as in Basic Chorale Style.

4. On half, dotted half and whole notes, also holds, in Full Chorale Style, the left hand can play an octave followed by a single bass note repeated an octave lower, if possible. In Basic Chorale Style, the left hand can play an octave followed by a chord or chords.

5. Accompaniment Style is used for hymns with moving melodies. The Time signatures of these hymns are usually $\frac{3}{4}$, $\frac{4}{4}$, and $\frac{6}{8}$.

6. In Accompaniment Style, the right hand will be the same as for Full Chorale Style but one octave higher than written. The left hand plays octaves on the strong beats and chords on the weak beats. Octaves are used in the left hand where there is a change of harmony within the measure.

7. If the right hand has a dotted note, the left hand does not play the dotted rhythm but keeps a steady beat with fill-ins. This is also done in Chorale Style. (There may be exceptions.) Usually, do not observe rests in the left hand but fill-in with some form of accompaniment for their time values.

8. Seventh chords in the right hand can be played in two ways when playing in either Full Chorale or Accompaniment Style:
    (a) Keep the soprano in octaves, but play four notes instead of five. Include the seventh tone of the chord as one of the notes.
    (b) Play the four different notes of the seventh chord leaving out the lower soprano note of the octave.

9. For hymns in $\frac{6}{8}$ and slow hymns in $\frac{3}{4}$ and $\frac{4}{4}$, usually play the left hand in eighth notes using octaves and chords. For the most part, keep the left hand moving at all times. Whenever there is a half or dotted half note in the right hand, play fill-in chords in quarter notes instead of holding the note. (Here again, there may be exceptions where it sounds better to hold the right hand while the left hand plays chords.)

10. Use passing tones and contrary motion in the left hand whenever possible to make the bass more interesting.

SECTION THREE

How To Play Hymns and Gospel Songs In Evangelistic Styles

In this section, a number of well-known and long-loved Gospel hymns are presented for your enjoyment. They have been arranged in Basic Chorale, Full Chorale, or Accompaniment Styles, or a combination of them, applying the principles taught in sections one and two.

Because of space, no introductions have been given. You are encouraged to add your own, using the suggestions on page 32.

The arrangement for each of these Gospel hymns is only one way of playing the hymn. Feel free to make changes, if you desire to do so. Happy playing!

Amazing Grace

(Basic Chorale Style)

JOHN NEWTON (1725 - 1807)

Early American Melody
Arr. by EDWIN O. EXCELL (1851 - 1921)

Stand Up, Stand Up For Jesus

(Full Chorale Style)

GEORGE DUFFIELD (1818 - 1888)

GEORGE J. WEBB (1803 - 1887)

Sweet By And By

(Accompaniment Style)

S. F. BENNET (20th Century)

J. P. WEBSTER (20th Century)

Throw Out The Lifeline
(Combining Basic Chorale and Accompaniment Styles)

EDWARD S. UFFORD (1851 - 1929)
Arr. by GEORGE C. STEBBINS (1846 - 1945)

Refrain:

FDL 760

Let The Lower Lights Be Burning

(Accompaniment Style)

PHILIP P. BLISS (1838 - 1876)

FDL 760

Beulah Land

(Accompaniment Style)

EDGAR PAGE STITES (1836 - 1921)

JOHN R. SWENEY (1837 - 1899)

view the shin - ing glo - ry-shore, My Heav'n, my home for - ev - er more!

The Old Time Religion

(Accompaniment Style)

Traditional

Chorus:

Give me that old - time re - lig-ion, Give me that old - time re - lig - ion,

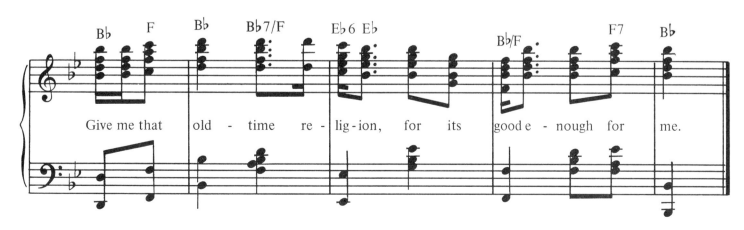

Give me that old - time re - lig-ion, for its good e - nough for me.

FDL 760

I Love To Tell The Story

(Accompaniment Style)

A. CATHERINE HANKEY (1834 - 1911)

WILLIAM G. FISCHER (1835 - 1912)

Rock Of Ages, Cleft For Me

(Full Chorale Style)

AUGUSTUS M. TOPLADY (1790 - 1778)   THOMAS HASTINGS (1784 - 1872)

FDL 760

O Happy Day

(Accompaniment Style - with few octaves)

PHILIP DODDRIDGE (1702 - 1751)　　　　　　EDWARD F. RIMBAULT (1816-1876)

Trust And Obey

(Basic Chorale Style)

JOHN H. SAMMIS (1846 - 1919)　　　　　　　　DANIEL B. TOWNER (1850 - 1919)

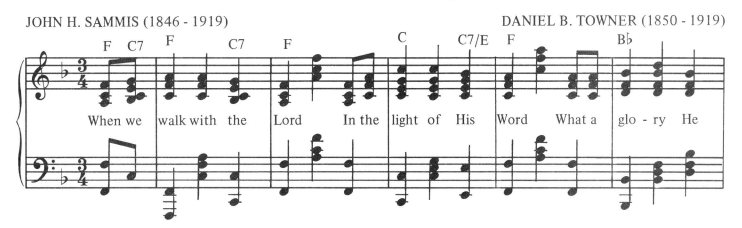

When we walk with the Lord In the light of His Word What a glo-ry He

sheds on our way! While we do His good will He a-bides with us still, And with

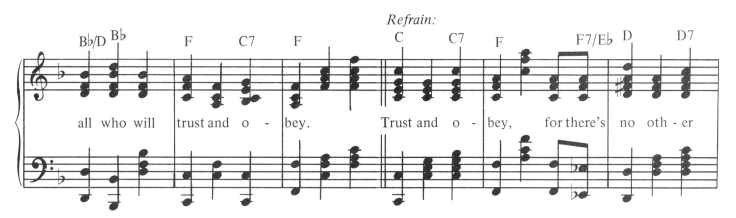

all who will trust and o-bey. Trust and o-bey, for there's no oth-er

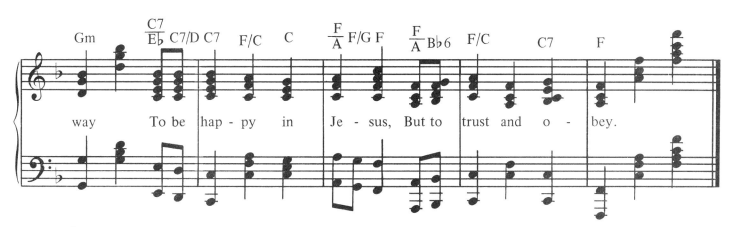

way To be hap-py in Je-sus, But to trust and o-bey.

FDL 760

We're Marching To Zion

(Accompaniment Style)

ISAAC WATTS (1674 - 1748)
Refrain by Robert Lowry

ROBERT LOWRY (1826 - 1899)

Come, we that love the Lord, And let our joys be known,

Join in a song with sweet ac - cord, Join in a song with sweet ac - cord,

And thus sur - round the throne, And thus sur-round the throne.

Refrain:

We're march - ing to Zi - on, Beau - ti-ful, beau - ti-ful Zi - on;

We're march-ing up-ward to Zi - on the beau-ti-ful ci -ty of God.

Revive Us Again

(Accompaniment Style)

WILLIAM P. MACKAY (1839 - 1885)　　　　　　　　　　　　　　JOHN J. HUSBAND (1760 - 1825)

We praise Thee, O God, for the Son of Thy love, For Je - sus who

died and is now gone a - bove.　*Refrain:* Hal - le - lu - jah! Thine the glo - ry, Hal - le -

lu - jah A - men; Hal - le - lu - jah! Thine the glo - ry; Re - vive us a - gain.

FDL 760

When The Roll Is Called Up Yonder
(Combining Basic Chorale and Accompaniment Styles)

JAMES M. BLACK (1856 - 1938)

Jesus Loves Me

(Basic Chorale Style)

ANNA B. WARNER (1820 - 1915) WILLIAM B. BRADBURY (1816 - 1868)

FDL 760

Shall We Gather At The River

(Basic Chorale Style)

ROBERT LOWRY (1826 - 1899)

Shall we gath-er at the riv - er, Where bright an-gel feet have trod;

With its crys-tal tide for-ev - er Flow-ing by the throne of God?

Refrain:

Yes, we'll gath - er at the riv - er, The beau-ti-ful, the beau-ti-ful riv - er,

Gath-er with the saints at the riv - er That flows by the throne of God.

There Shall Be Showers Of Blessing

(Accompaniment Style)

DANIEL W. WHITTLE (1840 - 1901)   JAMES McGRANAHAN (1840 - 1907)

FDL 760   *8va*

Blessed Assurance

(Accompaniment Style)

FANNY J. CROSBY (1820 - 1915)　　　　　　　　PHOEBE P. KNAPP (1839 - 1908)

The Church In The Wildwood

(Accompaniment Style)

DR. WILLIAM S. PITTS

There's a church in the valley by the wild - wood, No love - li - er spot in the dale;

No place is so dear to my child - hood As the lit - tle brown church in the vale.

Refrain:

Oh, come, come, come, come, Come to the church in the wild - wood, Oh come to the church in the

vale; No — spot is so dear to my child-hood As the lit - tle brown church in the vale.

FDL 760

When They Ring The Golden Bells

(Combining Basic Chorale and Accompaniment Styles)

DION DE MARBELLE

There's a land be-yond the riv-er, That we call the sweet for-ev-er, And we on-ly reach that shore by faith's de-cree; One, by one we'll gain the por-tals, There to dwell with the im-mor-tals, When they ring the gold - en bells for you and me.

Refrain:

Don't you hear the bells now ring-ing? Don't you hear the an - gels sing-ing? 'Tis the

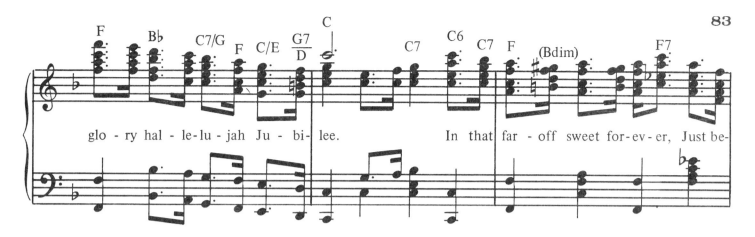

glo - ry hal - le - lu - jah Ju - bi - lee. In that far - off sweet for-ev-er, Just be-

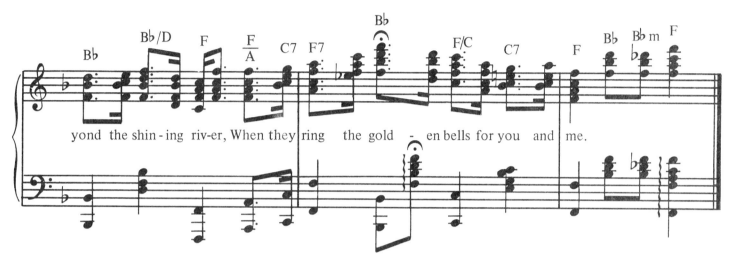

yond the shin - ing riv-er, When they ring the gold - en bells for you and me.

Jesus Loves The Little Children

(Accompaniment Style)

C. H. WOOLSTON

GEORGE F. ROOT (1820 - 1895)

Je - sus loves the lit - tle child - ren, All the child-ren of the world. Red or

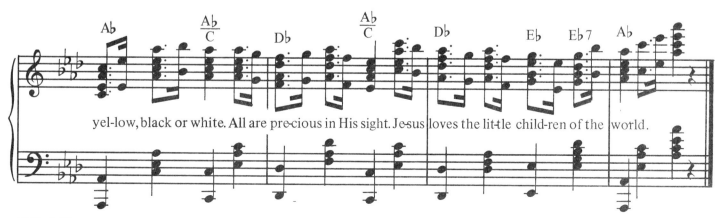

yel-low, black or white. All are pre-cious in His sight. Je-sus loves the lit-tle child-ren of the world.

FDL 760

Blest Be The Tie That Binds

(Accompaniment Style)

JOHN FAWCETT (1740 - 1817)

HANS G. NAGELI (1773 - 1836)
Arr. by LOWELL MASON (1792 - 1872)

When The Saints Go Marching In

(Accompaniment Style)

Traditional

FDL 760

Softly And Tenderly Jesus Is Calling

(Accompaniment Style)

WILL L. THOMPSON (1847 - 1909)

Soft - ly and ten - der - ly Je - sus is call-ing, Call-ing for you and for me;

See, on the por-tals He's wait-ing and watch-ing, Watch-ing for you and for me.

Refrain:

Come home, come home, Ye who are wea-ry, come home;

Ear - nest-ly, ten-der-ly, Je - sus is call-ing, Call - ing, O sin-ner, come home!

FDL 760

Wonderful Peace

(Accompaniment Style)

W. D. CORNELL (19th Century)   W. G. COOPER (19th Century)

o - ver my spir-it for - ev-er, I pray, In fath - om-less bil-lows of love.

Heavenly Sunshine

(Accompaniment Style)

H. J. ZELLY (20th Century)

GEORGE H. COOK (20th Century)

Refrain:

Heav-en - ly sun - shine, heav - en - ly sun - shine, Flood-ing my

soul with glo-ry di - vine;_____ Hal - le - lu jah! I am re -

joic - ing, Sing-ing His prais - es, Je - sus is mine.

FDL 760

Wonderful Words Of Life

(Accompaniment Style)

PHILIP P. BLISS (1838 - 1876)

Ring The Bells Of Heaven

(Basic Chorale Style)

WILLIAM O. CUSHING (1823 - 1902)   GEORGE F. ROOT (1820 - 1895)

FDL 760

Just As I Am, Without One Plea

Woodworth

(Basic Chorale Style)

CHARLOTTE ELLIOTT (1789 - 1871)

WILLIAM B. BRADBURY (1816 - 1868)

Am I A Soldier Of The Cross

Arlington

(Basic Chorale Style)

ISAAC WATTS (1674 - 1748)

THOMAS A. ARNE (1710 - 1778)

FDL 760

Leaning On The Everlasting Arms

(Combining Basic Chorale and Accompaniment Styles)

ELISHA A. HOFFMAN (1839 - 1929) ANTHONY J. SHOWALTER (1858 - 1924)

What a fel-low-ship, what a joy di-vine, Lean-ing on the ev-er-last-ing arms;

What a bless-ed-ness, what a peace is mine, Lean-ing on the ev-er-last-ing arms.

Refrain:

Lean - ing, lean - ing, Safe and se-cure from all a-larms;

Lean - ing, lean - ing, Lean-ing on the ev-er-last-ing arms.

FDL 760

Standing On The Promises

(Accompaniment Style)

R. KELSO CARTER (1849 - 1928)

Sweet Hour Of Prayer

(Accompaniment Style)

WILLIAM W. WALFORD (1772 - 1850)　　　　　WILLIAM B. BRADBURY (1816 - 1868)

Sweet hour of prayer, sweet hour of prayer, That calls me from a world of care,

And bids me at my Fa - ther's throne make all my wants and wish - es known;

In sea - sons of dis - tress and grief, My soul has oft - en found re - lief,

And oft es - caped the tempt - er's snare, By the re - turn, sweet hour of prayer.

FDL 760

Bring Them In

(Combining Basic Chorale and Accompaniment Styles)

ALEXCENAH THOMAS (19th Century)   WILLIAM A. OGDEN (1841 - 1897)

FDL 760

When He Cometh

Jewels

(Accompaniment Style)

WILLIAM O. CUSHING (1823 - 1902)　　　　　　　　GEORGE F. ROOT (1820 - 1895)

FDL 760

Jesus Loves Even Me

(Accompaniment Style)

PHILIP P. BLISS (1838 - 1876)